52
WAYS TO
STRETCH
A BUCK

Kenny Luck

OLIVER
NELSON

THOMAS NELSON PUBLISHERS
Nashville

To my precious
Christine and Cara

Published in Nashville, Tennessee, by Oliver-Nelson Books, a division of Thomas Nelson, Inc., Publishers, and distributed in Canada by Lawson Falle, Ltd., Cambridge, Ontario.

Printed in the United States of America.

Library of Congress Cataloging-in-Publication Data
Luck, Kenny, 1964–
    52 ways to stretch a buck / Kenny Luck.
      p. cm.
   ISBN 0-8407-9655-2 (paperback)
    1. Finance, Personal. 2. Saving and thrift. I. Title. II. Title: Fifty-two ways to stretch a buck.
HG179.L83   1992
332.024'01—dc20   92-17053
                                                      CIP

1 2 3 4 5 6 — 97 96 95 94 93 92

Contents

• Acknowledgments

Special thanks go first to Steve Arterburn for trusting me with this project. I am grateful for the opportunity and honored to be standing with you.

My wife, Chrissy, is clearly my heroine in life. Thank you for wearing a number of hats during a very busy time. You are the greatest wife, mother, friend, cook, and editor any person could have, and you are mine.

• Introduction

T he hunt is afoot!" These famous words from the young Sherlock Holmes are a fitting battle cry for this book. Instead of solving a mystery, however, this book will uncover ways to help you save money. All you have to do is join in, much like in an Easter egg hunt. The eggs are out there, and almost everyone will find at least one egg. This is my hope for you: that you find at least one savings concept that works for you. If you find more, great. And if you strike gold, fantastic!

What's great about Easter egg hunts is that no intrinsic or special talent is required. A person needs only eyes to see and a willingness to put them to use. If you are willing to take inventory of your spending and turn over a few rocky areas, you may be surprised at what you find.

52 Ways to Stretch a Buck sounds the whistle for financial planners and financial strugglers to join the hunt. Everyone is on equal turf. Look for the ideas that are easiest and most practical for *you*. Some you can implement right away, and others you will be able to use later. The key is to personalize each savings concept to your situation.

Employ your hunting skills. Good savers are very much like seasoned trackers. Cash savings may be found in obvious places you never bothered to notice, while others may be in the nooks and crannies of your daily spending. Fortunately, there's no time limit, and a good number of eggs are to be found.

It is my hope, as a fellow hunter, that you will come away with your share of eggs, have fun, and experience the satisfaction of a solid result. And perhaps, most important, I trust this book will help you discover other life principles that grow out of spending less money and spending more quality time with the people you love.

1 • Dealing for Dollars

Go to any gym these days, and you'll see it. Visit the weight-lifting section, and you'll hear it. Ask Mr. Olympia his secret, and he'll say it. Curious? I'm referring to the saying: NO PAIN, NO GAIN.

It is one of the most truthful, wise proverbs to grace the human mind. It can be applied to decision making, marriages, friendships, spiritual growth, bodybuilding, or any other worthwhile goal in life. It lets us in on a fundamental reality of life. That is, to improve, reach goals, and accomplish objectives, we must be willing to risk and sacrifice something.

Consumers would do well to understand and apply this principle when purchasing goods and services. Most consumers lose hundreds annually and thousands over the years because they are afraid to risk questioning the price tag or won't take time to do homework.

Achieving substantial savings through negotiation is simple and, in most cases, relatively painless.

It Never Hurts to Question the Price Tag   The main reason why it pays to haggle a little is that merchants are almost always motivated to keep sales volume up and inventory down. To this end, they are usually prepared to offer discounts between 20 and 40 percent on most items. Most consumers don't get a deal because they simply don't open their mouths and ask, "Can you do any better on this price?"

Information Is Leverage   Whether you're negotiating nuclear arms treaties or purchasing a luxury car, the more facts you know, the greater leverage you have, and the more likely you are to win out. Without solid information you are at the seller's mercy.

The bottom line is this: do a little homework if you want big savings.

- Compare.
- Get recommendations from others.
- Find out when new shipments arrive.
- Discover the best time to negotiate—end of the month, a certain season, rainy days, etc.

Remember, merchants will listen to a well-informed customer.

Never Be Afraid to Walk Away   No matter how much you want a certain item, sometimes it pays to say, "I appreciate the offer, but I'll have to think it over." Leave your name and number with the salesperson. You may be surprised at the result.

2 • Dinner for Two

Although eating out should be the exception and not the routine, a periodic dinner at a nice restaurant can be a breath of fresh air for couples with busy schedules. Husbands and boyfriends with a "certain other" they want to entertain can do it in style without draining their wallets. The first year of our marriage we discovered a little-used tool for saving money and promoting intimacy.

A friend told us to look in the paper for an advertisement for a new restaurant opening near us. We found it, cut it out, and put the two-for-one entrée offer to the test. The restaurant had an upscale look, but we weren't frightened off. We checked the menu, which seemed quite reasonable. Three courses later we walked out of there for less than $15, feeling pretty good about ourselves. It's a story worth repeating.

"Mmm Good" Savings The best place to find these coupons is in local papers. Next, look through the food section of a major newspaper. Last, watch your mail for regional coupon packs. If you are traveling, restaurant guides usually have a number of coupons from advertisers.

- Locate and cut out your coupons.
- Carefully read them to make sure your date doesn't conflict with any weekend or other restrictions. Make reservations if necessary.
- Make baby-sitter arrangements.
- Creatively inform your spouse of the night out. A Post-it Note on the mirror works for me. Let your date know of date, time, and dress requirements.
- When you arrive at the restaurant, check with the waiter to make sure you can use the coupon.
- Enjoy your meal and give your compliments to the chef.
- Tip as you would for the full price. The waiter served two people.

Saving on dinner makes "a dinner and a movie" night more affordable and, in a way, more special. Turning the tables on the cost of living can be a very satisfying feeling.

3 • Getting Command of Coupons

There they are, just sitting there waiting to be cut out. You're hesitating. You know using coupons will save you money, but are they worth the effort? You could easily rationalize a good case against clipping. Maybe you can't find your scissors, or the last time you went for a coupon in the kitchen drawer you couldn't find it. Let's assume you found the scissors and stored the coupons in an envelope, but then in the checkout line you realized you left the envelope at home. Even worse, the coupons you had painstakingly cut, saved, and brought to the store had expired. The results? Lost time, lost coupons, and embarrassment.

For those of you who are frustrated, reluctant, or otherwise unmotivated to embrace that slippery section of the paper again, there's hope. Don't give up just yet. Hundreds of dollars of savings are to be gained annually, and this chapter is going to help you get yours. The solution is a system that works.

This simple plan will help you significantly cut down on your grocery bills and eliminate most of the frustrating coupon quirks. Hang in there. Do you realize that even limited coupon use can save you over $100 a year easily? So whether you are in the major or minor leagues of couponing, you will benefit from something or everything that follows.

1. Where to Find Coupons

- The Sunday paper
- Specially marked packages
- Mail (open all your junk mail—you may be surprised to find out what you can save)
- Magazines
- Store circulars
- Food section in your local paper
- Coupon book (make sure the coupons can save you more than the cost of the coupon book)
- The store (check the bulletin board on your way into the market)

2. What Coupons Should You Cut?

Start small. Sometimes too many coupons produce clutter and end up being thrown away. Make a list of the items you regularly use and always cut coupons for those items. Then gradually add to your inventory to keep from becoming overwhelmed. Because saving cash is contagious, you will steadily increase this reserve and get better at using it.

3. Organize Your Coupons

Make it a system that works for you. First, decide on a method of storing and organizing your coupons. You can buy compact coupon files to fit in your purse or convert a shoe box into a coupon file box. Some people prefer envelopes labeled with the different categories. Next, decide how you will categorize your coupons: by food type, aisle number, or expiration date. Use whatever works best for you.

4. Don't Leave Home Without Them

Never leave home without your coupons. Keep them tucked away in your car. That way you have them when you need them and won't miss out on saving that cash.

5. Double Dollars

Shop where coupons are doubled. Some people shop at one store for the items they have double coupons for and then shop at another store with overall lower prices for the remainder of their grocery needs. Again, we're talking cash savings: one $0.50 coupon will be $1.00, two will be $2.00, and so on.

6. Monthly Inventory

At the beginning of the month, go through your inventory of coupons and pull all the coupons that expire that month. Build your menus around these items. Also, try to use your coupons when the item you need is already on sale. For instance, one week disposable diapers were $1.00 off the regular price of $10.99, and with a $1.00 coupon, which was doubled, we ended up saving $3.00.

7. Two Sunday Papers

If your Sunday paper has especially "hot" coupons, it might be a good idea to buy a couple of copies of the paper. However, make sure the savings will be greater than the cost of the extra newspaper.

8. When Not to Use a Coupon

Don't use a coupon if you can purchase another brand you like just as well and that is cheaper without one.

9. When to Buy Smaller or Bigger Sizes

When you use coupons, sometimes it is better to buy the smaller size since the savings are based on "cents off" instead of a percentage of the regular price. Take into consideration the price per unit for the regular price, the price per unit using a coupon, and the price per unit using a double coupon. Take a look at this price-per-unit comparison for Johnson's Baby Bath.

Item	Price	Unit Price	Coupon Amt.	Unit Price w/c	Unit Price w/double
9 oz.	$2.39	26.5¢	40¢	22.1¢	17.6¢
16 oz.	$3.89	24.3¢	40¢	21.8¢	19.3¢

In this case it is cheaper to buy the smaller size if the coupon can be doubled. If not, it would be more economical to buy the bigger size, and you would not need to replace the product as soon.

10. Gift Idea

Giving someone a collection of coupons not only costs nothing, but it will bring welcomed savings. Buy or make a coupon organizer, and fill it with coupons to fit the occasion. For a wedding, fill it with household coupons (i.e., for detergent, spices, canned goods, etc.). For a baby shower, coupons for diapers, baby wipes, bottles, nursery items, baby detergent, and so on are appropriate.

Saving coupons is one of the easiest ways to stretch your food dollar. With a good system you can easily save hundreds of dollars annually on your grocery bill. And that ain't peanuts.

4 • The Backyard Vacation

What is the measure of a good vacation? How you answer this question will reveal what part of your budget you'll need to commit to it. For some, it's the distance traveled. You know, getting away from it all. For others, the places where they stayed fuel their sense of status (real or imagined). "We stayed at the Biltmore." Still others will talk of where they ate or what they bought and brought home. These elements are surely part of the picture but certainly not all or even half of what makes a successful vacation.

These responses have two things in common. They all involve spending money, and they all fail to mention people. When I ask folks about their vacations, I am always amazed when they respond by rehearsing "things" and not sharing their experiences with others. Quality time spent with significant others is the measure of a good vacation and the signal that a vacation has accomplished its purpose for you and your family. Even better is the principle that the quality of the time spent is *not* contingent on the amount of money spent.

Quality Time Together Is Close to Home

The easiest way to plan a family vacation is to call a travel agent and let the agent do it all for you. However, the result will be added expenses and not necessarily a better vacation. The *best* person to plan your family vacation is you.

- Check with local, state, and nearby states' offices of tourism as well as your travel agent for information. Consider state or national parks, beaches, and other outdoor-oriented locations. If vacationing outdoors is not your style, consider nearby cities and areas rich in culture and tradition. Festivals operate year-round in cities in America, and each has its own emphasis and activities.
- Narrow the choices to three locations, and present the different places and possible activities to your family to decide. This is the first shared experience of your vacation.
- Make your selection of possible locations close enough to travel by car or even by train. Traveling by train is not only less expensive than flying, but getting there is more enjoyable and memorable for the kids.

Planning to Save on Your Trip

Once the family has chosen a location, make general plans for lodging, food, range of activities, and expenses. Then plan and prepare to save.

One of the easiest ways to save on vacations is

to travel with other families or relatives. Up to 75 percent of your travel cost can be cut, and 60 to 75 percent of lodging can be saved. Be sure, however, you get along well with the people you are joining.

Pack a special bag or duffle of assorted snacks, juices, and fruit to eat while traveling. You will cool off big appetites and save on fast-food dollars.

Try to find lodging with a kitchenette. You can shop locally and prepare easy meals like spaghetti, burritos, soup and sandwiches, and so on. Your travel agent can help you find the lowest rate for your need. If appropriate and possible, stay with relatives a day or two.

Plan activities based on family participation and interaction. Biking, hiking, visiting museums, boat riding, sledding, fishing, skiing, touring special historical sights—often these activities cost less than amusement parks, which may be enjoyable for the little kids but not for the big ones. Focus on making memories.

Along this line, taking pictures or videotaping your trip will solidify a memorable vacation as you relive your trip in later years.

5 • Month-to-Month Money

The wheels of commerce turn with predictable regularity on an annual basis. The key is timing your purchases.

January   Traditional after-Christmas and New Year's bargains include men's suits, linens (white sales), appliances, and furniture.

February   The season of love brings big reductions on china, glass, silver, mattresses, and bedding.

March   Watch for special preseason promotions for spring clothing. Ski equipment is at an annual low as well.

April   Sales begin again after the Easter holiday, especially on clothing.

May   Spring cleaning means specials on household cleaning products. This also is a good month to shop for carpets and rugs.

June   Shop for furniture. Semiannual inventory is on its way in, and old items must go.

July   Most stores liquidate their inventories to make room for fall goods during this month. Sportswear, sporting equipment, and garden tools and supplies take noticeable dips.

August   If you are in the market for a car, August is clearance time on current models. Also, equipment linked to the summer season is marked down. Look for good deals on patio furniture, lawn mowers, yard tools, and barbecue and camping equipment.

September   The best deals on school clothes are at the *end* of the month. If you can hold off the "first day complex," you'll save big on what's in this year.

October   This is *the* month to do your Christmas shopping. Stores are postured to boost retail sales before the holiday season.

November   Wool clothes from women's coats to men's suits come down significantly this month as store owners cut their inventories for their second shipment of the season.

December   Next to August, this month is the best time to buy a new car.

6 • "Mom and Dad: Send Money!"

Have you ever noticed when they pan the crowd at college football games that in addition to screaming fans and the spirited banners you see signs with "Mom and Dad: Send Money!"? The image of the penny-pinching American college student seems to be imbedded in our national psyche.

Your average starving student profile is the self-motivated, nonscholarshiped student who has little or no family support and must work his or her way through school. If this description fits you or your child, holding up signs at football games may have a legitimate place. If not, we need to know where and how we can stretch Mom and Dad's dollars.

Room and Board   Having a place to sleep and eat are universal expenses. The college freshman must adjust to new systems for both. Dormitories, dorm food, fraternities, sororities, campus apartments, and eating on your own are part and parcel of the college experience. Unless you're commuting from home, you want to avail yourself of every opportunity for saving in these areas.

Dormitories   Dormitories are usually the best deal for room and board. Most campuses have it down to a science in terms of housing and feeding hundreds of students efficiently. Because the dorms are administered by the school, they normally cost significantly less than housing in the private sector. Meals are served three times a day, which saves the student from having to shop for and prepare meals. If it's at all possible, stay in campus housing to save money.

Fraternities and Sororities   Many students find the experience with the Greek system enjoyable, and their parents like the bottom line. On many campuses, low monthly rent and an affordable meal plan make fraternities and sororities financially appealing. Finances aside, students must evaluate if this environment would best serve their educational and personal goals.

Off-Campus Housing   Finding roommates is the key to saving money on off-campus housing. For example, six young men lived in a three-bedroom apartment. They divided the rent by six and shared certain meals (breakfast most often). An added benefit is forming strong friendships that last long beyond college days.

Food   Grocery shopping and cooking are not factors in the dorms or in a fraternity or sorority, but they are new responsibilities for students living in apartments. Here are some tips for saving on your food expenses at school.

- Try to bring groceries from home. Merchants in college towns are keenly aware of their captive market. Students will pay for convenience, so stock up on items that last and are easy to fix, such as soups, pastas, macaroni packages, cereal, bagels, muffin mixes, peanut butter, frozen chicken, and so on.
- If you need to shop at school, make the effort to go off-campus for big orders. You'll be amazed at prices a couple of miles down the road.

Laundry   Do your laundry at home. Coin-operated machines are costly and must be baby-sat. Laundromats are subject to crowding.

If you have to use the Laundromat, wash full loads of whites and colors together in warm water and your darks and bright colors in cold. Fewer loads mean less money.

Dry only full loads. But don't overload or your clothes will remain damp.

Utilities   The one utility that no landlord covers is the telephone bill. A system is appropriate for this utility because unclaimed calls on the bill can be sources of frustration and contention. The person whose name is on the bill must explain at the outset the courtesies that must be afforded by roommates when the bill arrives. They involve

- individually reviewing the bill and claiming calls.
- keeping a log of long-distance calls made.
- reimbursing the roommate responsible for paying the bill well in advance of the due date.

Encouraging a Mind-Set   College is a great opportunity for young adults to learn money management principles. Parents can set the pace by working through a spending plan with a student and encouraging the benefits of being thrifty.

7 • Being Together

What is the purpose of a date?

If you are not married, generally the purpose of a date is to get to know someone better. If you are married, that is part of it, but you can add a well-deserved break from the kids and time out to re-establish communication or romantic intimacy. The common thread is just being together.

The only problem with dates these days is that you have to drain your bank account. Costs for dinner for two and a movie aren't what they used to be. Being together is now a $20 to $40 expense every time. And since the need to meaningfully be together will never go away (or shouldn't), we need to be creatively economical.

A Meaningful Date   Doing the things you did after you first met is a good guideline for a successful date: holding hands, hanging on your date's every comment or word (listening), being playful, and sharing secrets. Also important is any other expression that brings you back to the central point: I'm glad I'm with you right now. And although all this sounds good, sometimes you need a jump start—some activity or location that puts those feelings back in your heart by tapping into specific memories or experiences.

In college, one couple went to a cafe that served wonderful desserts, cappuccinos, and flavored coffees on an outdoor patio. They would sit, share a piece of cake, sip coffee, and talk. It was a perfect date for a college student's budget.

Today the venue has changed, but the tradition lives on. Now they go to a cafe with an outdoor patio on a lake. Every time they go there something just takes over. Of course, they are married and have a family now, but it's still got that magic. The "dessert date" will be with them the rest of their lives. No matter what their financial status, they'll always have a meaningful, inexpensive way to be together.

The dessert date accomplishes the purpose of a date without the enormous expense. They eat dinner at home, find a baby-sitter for a few hours, and then save dessert for the date. They'll spend $6 to $10 on something that's worth $1 million in the relationship. And isn't that usually the way it works? The best things in life are free (or relatively inexpensive). Quality time is usually cheap.

Ask yourself, Where did the magic start for us? Where did we go? What did we do? It's a good bet your wallet was a little thinner then, and it didn't matter.

8 • Painless Savings

Where has all the money gone?

Cups of coffee, video rentals, lunches with co-workers, Girl Scout cookies, take-out suppers, and countless other transactions are unplanned expenses that are hard to keep track of on a regular basis. Money back from your tens and twenties slips through your fingers like sand, and when tax time comes, you scratch your head in amazement. Where did all that money go?

When you live paycheck to paycheck (and I know what that's like), your savings just don't seem to shake hands with reality. Or so it seems. Even if you think you can't spare the money, you can start to build a savings account without experiencing the emotional sting of letting the money go. Sound too good to be true? That's the beauty of implementing an automatic savings plan with only 5 percent of your income.

You will find that nothing will change in your day-to-day life. The difference will be that the money that was imperceptibly disappearing will now be earning interest. Life will go on the same as usual, and savings will become a reality.

Sign Me Up!   Ask your employer about a payroll deduction plan and sign up. Commit 5 percent of your income to the plan. If you don't have payroll savings, arrange with your bank to transfer money from checking to savings every month. Eventually, plan to go to 7 percent and then to 10 percent.

9 • Root for the Home Team

In the movie *Hoosiers,* the story traces the state of Indiana's affection for high-school basketball and how it can get too intense for the community and the players. Though this is a subtheme, it is not what you remember from the movie. What sticks is the thrill of vicariously getting to know a group of young athletes and following their odyssey all the way to the state championship. It's an inspirational story.

Firsthand Experience Though Hollywood's ability to parallel real life is often wanting, it succeeded in this case. High-school sports in certain areas of the country are more popular than professional sporting events. In fact, my wife and I experienced "the fever" firsthand and really got into it when we lived in Plano, Texas. There was just something about eleven thousand screaming fans cheering on the kids who don't play for money. It's all about family, sense of community, and the excitement of competition that get you there and keep you coming back.

Initially, we were cool to the idea. But it took just one game, and we were hooked. The best thing about it is that you don't have to be sports conscious to take advantage of the fun. A friend takes his seven-year-old son to local games so that they can spend time together and share a common interest. This friend views high-school sports as a form of preteen entertainment for his son.

Go Team!   One benefit of these events is that the cost for tickets is a fraction of that of pro events and cheaper than the price for a movie ticket for adults. Kids often get in free. High-school sporting events are particularly appropriate for children ages seven through twelve or whenever they are beginning to play the same sports.

So if you need an entertainment outlet for your kids and want to stretch a dollar:

- Call the school and inquire about the sports schedule and ticket costs.
- Play the sport ahead of time to orient or prime your kids for the game.
- The day of the game, plan a fast-food meal or dessert after the game to begin a tradition.
- Play ball!
- Follow the team in the newspaper. That's a great way to get your children interested in current events and reading.

10 • Getting Fit for a Bargain

Imagine the sounds of music and clapping coming from a church basement. Clapping? Yes, clapping—and not in response to a stirring message from the pastor. It is uniform and multiplied in number. What is going on? An exercise class!

These people have discovered a fitness savings concept that encourages them to have a blast. In fact, aerobics classes, weight training, and fitness programs facilitated through churches and community centers pay off in both respects.

Many people who have embraced the fitness life-style are paying monthly fees at health clubs that amount to hundreds annually. And a high percentage of them do not attend regularly.

Research at the University of Connecticut revealed both the economic and the motivational advantages of community-based fitness programs. Not only do you save hundreds annually on membership fees, but researchers say you will attend more faithfully. Their research showed that community-based fitness provides the motivation and close-knit environment that for-profit clubs are missing.

How Can I Tell If This Kind of Program is Appropriate For Me?

Ask yourself,

- Is regular exercise of interest to me?
- Am I currently paying for a fitness club membership?
- Do I need to increase my cash flow?
- Does my church or community center have fitness programs operating?
- Would any of my friends be interested in signing up with me?

If you answered yes to any of these questions, you should consider a community-based fitness program. Call your church and inquire about any fitness groups and the times they meet. If your church does not have a program, look up your local community center or YMCA as an alternative resource.

What If I Am Presently a Member of a Club?

If you are financing a health club membership, some companies will allow you to opt out of your contract by paying a certain percentage of your remaining balance. Call the finance company and inquire. Don't wait. Get fit for a bargain and enjoy the experience more!

11 • Baby-Sitting Co-Op

A blue-ribbon panel of mothers talked about family life, creative parenting, and how to handle various parenting roadblocks. After a stimulating discussion on potty training, they tackled baby-sitting. One of the panel members explained the advantages of co-op baby-sitting for mothers of infants, toddlers, preschoolers, and elementary school-age children. The mothers can have a day out during the week to pamper themselves, shop, exercise, or run much-needed errands.

There are many advantages to co-op baby-sitting, and the financial benefits are clear. It costs little, if anything, to carry out. Here's how it works.

What Is a Baby-sitting Co-op?

It is a group of mothers who trade off watching one another's children on a rotating, mutually agreed-upon basis. Mothers have a choice between evening or day care and pay nothing. Services are bartered, creating the co-op nature of the system.

How Do I Start a Baby-sitting Co-op?

Poll close acquaintances who have children to gauge interest. You will need a minimum of two and a maximum of four mothers for a workable co-op.

Meet with mothers at least two weeks before the co-op starts to determine a schedule and agree to which periods the co-op will recess (Saturdays, holidays, etc.). Fill out your chart for the first month, and then meet the third week of each consecutive month to fill out the next schedule.

Establish general guidelines for everyone to follow so that no one is taken advantage of or misunderstands the commitment. For example, mothers may choose daytime or nighttime care for their day out, range of acceptable hours to be gone, and so on.

Rotate leadership of the co-op planning meetings among participating members. A co-op leader is responsible for calling members to remind them of their meeting and for recording the schedule for anyone who can't be there.

What Are the Do's?

- Always leave a phone number.
- Always call to check in.
- Bring something for your child to do (a favorite doll, video, etc.).
- Leave food or a treat of some kind for the co-op sitter.

What Are the Don'ts?

- Don't expose a sick child to other children. Take a rain check.
- Don't be late for sitting assignments. Mothers will have very wisely planned their use of time.
- Don't bring messy toys to another's house (Play-Doh, coloring pens, etc.).

What Are the Advantages of Co-op Baby-sitting?

- Encourages marital intimacy as a way of life and structures it into a marriage.
- Emphasizes mutual support, community, and service to others.
- Develops strong bonds of friendship with members.
- Provides excellent care for children. Who better to watch your infant than an experienced mother?
- Saves money.

What If I Don't Know Any Mothers?

- You could sign up for a Mommy and Me Class in your community to meet other mothers.
- You could put an ad in the church bulletin.
- Or you could put a note in your community newsletter.

Baby-Sitting Co-Op

Schedule for _____ (month)

Week 1: Days 6–11
S M T W *Th* F S
Day Out For: Luck
Baby-Sitter: Genoway
Time: 6:00 P.M.–10:00 P.M.

Week 2: Days 12–17
S M Tu *W* Th F S
Day Out For: Genoway
Baby-Sitter: Hoover
Time: 12:00 P.M.–4:00 P.M.

Week 3: Days 19–24
S M *Tu* W Th F S
Day Out For: Hoover
Baby-Sitter: Luck
Time: 10:00 A.M.–2:00 P.M.

Week 4: Days 26–31
S M Tu W Th *F* S
Day Out For: Luck
Baby-Sitter: Genoway
Time: 1:00 P.M.–5:00 P.M.

12 • Auto Insurance Treasure

Sometimes savings are right under our noses, but we don't know it. We just write out our checks and put them in the mail. We can save hundreds by learning the components of our auto insurance policies and making a basic assessment of our needs.

The first step is learning what protection you definitely need. A standard package will include the following coverage:

- Bodily injury
- Property damage
- Collision damage
- Comprehensive
- Uninsured motorist bodily injury
- Medical or personal injury protection

Advisers recommend that you not compromise on bodily injury and property damage categories. They suggest coverages of $100,000 to $300,000 for bodily injury and $50,000 for property damage. Savings are discovered by determining the other areas that you can adjust or eliminate.

Collision and Comprehensive   Sometimes this represents 40 percent of the premium with deductibles ranging from $50 to $1,000. Deductibles are what you pay out of your pocket before the insurance kicks in. Choosing high deductibles can lower your premiums significantly. Each $100 increase in your collision deductible will lower your premium cost 7 to 15 percent. The same $100 increase for comprehensive has a corresponding drop of 15 to 30 percent in your premium cost.

Uninsured Motorist Bodily Injury   Since this coverage can range from $30,000 per person (with a $60,000 maximum payout) up to $100,000 per person (with a $300,000 maximum payout), it can represent $30 to $70 each premium. To determine the limits, consider the sources of protection you already have. Look upon this coverage as supplemental protection to a full-range income protection and medical expense program. Consider the following:

- income source. A self-employed person may need more protection than a person employed by a large conglomerate.
- medical care coverage from employment sources.
- the portion of income derived from investments, pensions, and annuities.

Medical Coverage   If you have life and/or health insurance, your medical coverage will probably be unnecessary. If so, you can save up to another $100 per year.

Personal Injury Protection   The same application for medical coverage works here. If your health benefits indicate that the carrier will be the primary payer for accident-related medical bills, you could cut these costs by 40 percent.

Car Rental Reimbursement   If you have two cars, you should reconsider keeping this item on your policy.

Towing Insurance   If you belong to an auto club, you don't need it.

New Car   If you are buying a new car, choose a model with a history of few insurance claims. The Institute for Highway Safety in Alexandria, Virginia, can send you information. Cars with favorable claim histories save you as much as $200 annually, because they demonstrate low repair costs resulting from accidents.

Discounts   Ask about discounts for which you may qualify.

13 • Anniversaries

It has been said that *love* is really spelled *t-i-m-e*. Saying, "I love you," lacks power without a proportional investment of time to back it up. It's that simple. So when we say we don't have time for something, we are not so much stating a fact as a priority. The message is clear. Our children know it, and our spouses know it.

Unfortunately, our culture has successfully replaced quality time and its inherent message with quick fixes. Our high-tech low-touch culture has alienated people from one another, especially marriage partners. Not only is this downward spiral in relating between husbands and wives unhealthy, but men usually try to medicate this problem with their wallets. It's a common scenario.

The husband waits until the last minute to plan the anniversary. So he calls to make a dinner reservation at a nice restaurant and maybe purchases a gift. Perhaps he will even make hotel reservations. For the sake of argument, let's increase this husband's stock and say that he delivers her one red rose to start the day off and a card, too. Out of all these anniversary happenings, what will his wife remember first? Most men would point to where they spent the most money. Most women would mention the one red rose. Why? Because it sends the most meaningful message.

The most successful anniversaries are heavy on thoughtful planning and light on money. A dozen red roses, candy, expensive restaurants, hotels, and gifts are no substitutes for planning how you are going to spend time together and ultimately spending the time. A well-planned anniversary can do wonders for a marriage. For your next anniversary, resolve to spend less money and more time in the planning and time together on "your day." Here are some helpful tips on how to do both.

Planning a Successful Anniversary

Make a large note on the calendars at home and in the office signaling your anniversary. Make a second note to yourself in your personal planner one month ahead of time: "Plan for our anniversary."

Here is a sample plan.

1. List your spouse's favorite things to do:

- Going out to breakfast
- Shopping (supply a modest amount of money for her to spend)
- Going out for coffee

- Taking a walk in the woods or on the beach
- Eating at a favorite restaurant

2. Select two or three items on your list and plan to spend significant time doing the things your spouse likes to do.

3. Plan to spend an entire day together. Either take a day off or purpose to spend a Saturday together.

4. Make arrangements for the kids. This is one day you can model a healthy commitment to your spouse. Explain to them why you celebrate this day and that when they are married, they will, too.

5. Keep your spouse in the dark about your activities for the day. Let her discover for herself your thoughtful planning.

If you are staying at a hotel, check on package deals that often include dinner and breakfast. They will save you money.

14 • Money Marketing

Isuzu was onto something when the company manufactured a car and called it the Impulse. The name suggests freedom from care and excitement at the same time. Many American consumers get excited or otherwise motivated to buy something and spend freely. In fact, being uninhibited with money is encouraged by our culture as a virtue. Could it be that the managers knew this when they named the car? If you are determined to save money at the market, you are going to have to go against the grain.

Families must be fed, houses must be cleaned, hair must be washed, sinks need unclogging, and on and on. Marketing in this sense is a lifelong activity you can't get around. And yet, many of us continue to waste hundreds of dollars a year making these trips when, with very little effort, we could be saving that money.

If you could save $10 to $25 every time you make a trip to the market and you average one trip a week, conservatively speaking, that would add up to $520 in one year. Ask yourself, How many times do I go to the market per week? How much do I save each trip?

Money Marketing Procedures

If you have ninety minutes to give in return for hundreds in annual savings, here is a plan to use to start saving this week.

- Clip, organize, and use coupons. Make it a habit *not* to shop without them. Resource your Sunday paper, women's magazines, mailings, and grocery store circulars and coupons to build your reserve.
- After reading store circulars and looking over your coupons, plan a menu for the entire week.
- Make your marketing list from your menu for the week. Never shop without a list; it will keep you from impulse buying.
- Pull out and organize your coupons according to the layout of the store.
- Shop quickly. Research shows that after the first half hour consumers spend an average of $0.75 per minute.

After your first trip, plug your savings into the annual savings formula and see how money marketing will pay off for you.

AMOUNT SAVED/WEEK	WEEKS/YEAR	TOTAL ANNUAL SAVINGS
_____ ×	52	= _____

15 • Flirting with Debt

Debt is like an old girlfriend or boyfriend who won't stop calling. It's as if debt asked you out on a date, you agreed, and now you regret having said yes in the first place. You are trying to get on with your life, but every month you are confronted with the consequence of your choice. If there is one relationship you wish could end, it's this one.

The problem is that you are finding it difficult to cut the ties completely. You like to flirt with debt even though your experience with it tells you it's not a good thing. It has its tentacles around you, and you can't seem to break away.

One Step Forward, Two Steps Back

When trying to free yourself from debt, you feel that you're in a losing battle. You are fighting a mental battle between the need to save and the need to pay off your debt. You don't feel good about not having money in savings for emergencies, but on the other hand, you need to reduce your debt. Since most of us can't finance an emergency, we opt for cash in the bank and lose ground on eliminating our debt. The problem with this approach to finances is that the difference between interest rates for savings accounts and credit cards causes us to lose more than we gain. For example, your savings account may be paying you 6 percent interest while your credit card account is charging you 15 to 21 percent over the same period.

Two Steps Forward, No Steps Back

One way to successfully deal with your debt is a consolidation plan. It is very simple. You get a loan or a home equity line of credit at a low interest rate to completely pay off your debt. This move can save you the hundreds you may have been losing annually as well as put you in a position to break debt's grip on your finances. Consult your bank or financial planner to see which consolidation plan is best for you.

Don't Get Sidetracked

One of the detours for people who have gotten themselves back on the road to financial freedom is nonmonthly expenses that require large chunks of cash: car insurance premiums, car registrations, medical or dental emergencies, car repairs, and so on. These disturbances snowball into your spending plan and wipe it out.

Staying on the right track means you need to plan for these expenses. Once you have figured out your annual commitments to these categories, you can put a plan into action that helps you save the right amount each month. So the next time these bills come up, the money is there. I call it a money fund—a separate checking account exclusively for these expenses and emergencies.

Little by Little   Small deposits over time will build a solid savings account. The key to saving and getting out of debt is putting a small percentage (5 percent or so) of your monthly income away regularly. Dramatic deposits to bolster savings usually result in dramatic withdrawals. Consistency over time will build your confidence as well as your savings.

16• Open to the Public

One Friday afternoon John came home from his daily run and asked, "So what's the plan?" In response, his wife held up a clipping from the newspaper, which read, "An Old Town Christmas." Three hours later John was at an event open to the public.

Committed to having a terrible time, he showed up, put on a good face, and got caught up into a memorable experience. Crafts, food, carols, period actors, carriages, exhibits, and a crisp winter night captured the season. Ever since then, John's attitude toward public events has changed. Not only did he and his wife have a great time, but they didn't have to spend much money. While there is an appreciable risk in attending an event without the benefit of a recommendation or past experience, the thrill of discovering a winner is worth it. Public events are goodwill efforts designed to garner a sense of community and service. This ingredient lends itself directly to the quality of the time spent as well as to a freedom from having to spend money.

Variety   If you receive a daily newspaper, the Friday paper will usually feature a calendar of the weekend's community events. Many are free, and you will be pleasantly surprised at what is available. Community events include the following:

- Arts/crafts fairs
- Music festivals and concerts (classical, jazz, etc.)
- Art exhibits
- Athletic clinics
- Film festivals for kids
- Cultural fairs
- Airshows
- Seasonal dramatic productions
- Parades
- Carnivals

Reduced Expenses   Although most excursions will involve some expense, public events let you determine the level of spending and the amount of time you will invest. What's more, many events can be educational and interactive for children. In this way, families can make meaningful memories and begin traditions without the expense and planning of vacations. As we are discovering, many times the best things in life are free.

17 • Bargains Off the Beaten Path

Garage sales, flea markets, consignment shops, and thrift stores are treasure chests waiting to be discovered. Their function is best explained by the common saying, "One person's junk is another person's treasure." Just at the time when a piece of furniture or a decoration has worn out its welcome in one place, it finds a second life in the hands of another individual or family. Most items bought off the beaten path have a very specific function for the buyer. So whether you're a collector or a dad needing furniture for a playhouse or a mom who wants to liven up a home, these are the places you should check out.

What Can You Find?   Here is a short list of things commonly found at garage sales and consignment shops:

- Kitchen tables/ chairs
- Old signs
- Period jewelry
- Decorative old books
- Toys
- Board games
- Stereo components
- Bed frames
- Headboards
- Secretary desks
- Work desks

- Couches
- Clothes
- Love seats
- Armchairs
- Armoires
- Bookcases
- Sports equipment
- China sets
- Christmas decorations
- Glassware
- Tools
- Lamps
- Small appliances
- Silver
- Period clothing

Not only are these items sold at a fraction of retail, but many will complement your existing furniture or home in unique ways. Other items can be turned into projects and with a little effort and paint can be winning pieces for you.

What Are Your Needs Around the House?

Perhaps you could benefit from bargains off the beaten path.

Check the telephone directory and classified section in the paper to locate stores and garage sales.

Ask yourself, What do I keep telling myself I need but don't want to spend the money on? Or take a walk around your home to get ideas and remind yourself of some things you want to look for.

Make your hunting list. It could look something like this:

- Rocker for Chrissy (baby coming)
- Dresser for Cara

- Tool set for Kenny
- Everyday dishes for cabin
- Decorations for mantel in living room

Hit the trail. Wear comfortable clothes and plan on spending a few hours driving and walking.

Before you purchase something, be sure to handle it to check for durability, safety, and so on.

18 • It's Black and White but Not Read

In our fast-paced, remote control, push-button, automated teller society, taking the time to read the paper for a bargain may require a seat belt for many people. The problem is that in our drive to save time, we usually don't save money. And for those of you who have never thoroughly looked through your local or daily paper to see what your neighbors want to sell you at a cheap price, you don't know what you're missing.

Just taking the time to look in the paper could end up saving you two to five times the retail price of many items. So if what you seek doesn't absolutely, positively have to come from a showroom or store shelf, someone close by probably has what you need and wants to sell it to you. One of the best returns on investment is the quarter you pay for a newspaper.

Seek and Ye Shall Find a Bargain   A quick look in my newspaper revealed deals on the following items:

- Armoires
- Bassinets
- Bathroom scales
- Bench presses

- Bicycles
- Bird cages
- Boats
- Bookcases
- Bunk beds
- Camcorders
- Carpet
- Cars
- Cats
- Cellular phones
- China
- Clarinets
- Cockatoos
- Computers
- Copiers
- Diamonds
- Dishes
- Dogs
- Dollhouses
- Dryers
- Dumbbells
- Electric guitars
- Electric trains
- Exercise bikes
- Fax machines
- Fishing rods
- Four-poster beds
- Golf clubs
- Jacuzzis
- Jukeboxes
- Ladders
- Lawn mowers
- Love seats
- Mattresses
- Microwaves
- Office furniture
- Organs
- Outboard motors
- Patio furniture
- Persian rugs
- Pianos
- Refrigerators
- Rolltop desks
- Saxophones
- Scuba gear
- Ski equipment
- Sofas
- Tool sets
- Trading cards
- Trailer hitches
- Treadmills
- Trombones
- Trumpets
- TV sets
- Typewriters
- VCRs
- Video games
- Violins
- Washing machines
- Wedding dresses
- Wheelchairs

19 • Family Energy Savings Plan

One memory sure to get a chuckle in many families is mention of Dad's penchant for turning off lights. Most dads were like energy watchdogs. And when a child would leave a light on after leaving the room, a dad's common refrain would be, "Lights cost money." And he would turn them off.

Household energy and utilities can make up a significant part of the family budget. Instead of burdening Mom and Dad with the "utility police" stigma, a family-based energy/utility plan can help you reign in this area of your budget and accomplish other family goals as well. It involves everyone, teaches adolescents concepts of stewardship and reward, and ultimately saves you money on your bills. Here's how it works.

Family Meeting   Call a family meeting or use the evening meal as a forum to bring up the energy savings plan. Explain that if the family saves money on energy and utilities, the money can be applied to a specific area that benefits the entire family. You can apply a fixed monthly figure to allowances, videos for the family library, trips, and so on.

Assign each family member an area of responsibility. For example, an adolescent daughter will be in charge of phone use by the family. It will be her responsibility to remind family members of time limits when using the phone. Other family assignments can include these:

- Dad—Thermostat monitor
- Mom—Gas monitor
- Daughter—Light and appliance monitor
- Son—Shower and water monitor
- Other member—phone monitor

Duties   The *thermostat monitor* makes sure the thermostat is at 65° to 70° in winter months, 75° to 80° in summer months; the person closes vents in unused rooms. The *gas monitor* watches for and encourages efficient use of gas appliances in the home. Gas stoves and dryers are two primary examples. Assign this post to whomever does most of the cooking and laundry in the home. Many times using the microwave is more cost-efficient and takes less time than a gas stove. Drying full loads cuts gas costs when doing laundry. The *light and appliance monitor* watches for appliances being left on—TV, stereo, radio, and so on. The *shower monitor* makes sure family members don't become water slugs and drive up the water bill. The *phone monitor* watches out for "phone hogs."

You can add incentives by challenging monitors to find ways to save in their areas with specific benefits for them related to their ideas. Assignments can alternate monthly. Mom and Dad will find out what is saved, and the family will decide how to spend the savings.

Parents must abide by the family's commitment. So while the plan is largely instructional for children, it requires parents to "walk the walk" as well as "talk the talk" so that the entire family benefits. Depending on the size of your family and dwelling, monitors can save you $20 to $100 a month.

20 • Dessert Warfare

This chapter is not on strategic battle tactics or the Gulf War. The title is just a play on words and a fitting name for a group entertainment plan that promises lots of fun, food, and possibly a little warfare as husbands, wives, couples, and friends playfully square off. It's high-quality time at a low price. More than that, it cultivates community and builds bonds of friendship by creating a memorable shared experience.

The Time   To cut down on the amount of effort and money, plan the evening to start around 8:00 P.M. Friends can eat a leisurely dinner without having to rush over to the host's house.

The Food   The host supplies one dessert, coffee, and plates and silverware. The guests agree to bring a dessert. Since people have already eaten dinner, serve dessert as a type of intermission.

The Entertainment   A number of group entertainment games for adults can be used. Every once in a while, have a night of multiple games with a point system for individuals or couples to score and win. Some games that work well for group entertainment are Scattergories, Personal Preference, Outburst, and Charado, Pictionary, or Guestures.

To put a cap on the evening, you can rent a video classic for everyone to enjoy.

Playing the Games   Sometimes the element of competition can be overdone. However, other times a healthy battle can be a natural mixer for your guests so that they get to know one another in the context of playing a game.

Because some guests may be unfamiliar with the games you have selected, it is always helpful to explain how to play a certain game and also play a "practice round."

Number of Guests   Because most games restrict the number of players, limit guests to ten or less. You may have the best dessert spread in town, but it requires a lot of effort to catch the attention of a larger group when you want to get the evening under way.

An Evening of Dessert Warfare   Poll your friends by telephone or written invitation for this informal get-together. Communicate the date and time. Instruct them to bring a suitable game for a large group.

Plan your evening.

- Serving drinks and having chitchat—
  8:00–8:15
- Game(s) of choice—8:30–9:30
- Dessert intermission/cooling off—
  9:30–10:00
- Game(s) of choice or video—10:00–11:00

Twists You Can Add   After dessert, the group can walk off calories by taking a stroll together. It stimulates conversation and is good for digestion.

You can end your evening on a spiritual note by sharing prayer requests and praying for one another. You never know who may be hurting in the group and could really use the support.

21 • Teaming Up on the Holidays

The spirit of the holidays brings us back home. There is something about the season that draws family and friends together in a unique way. Here are a few suggestions to help you survive the holidays, build friendships, and save dollars.

Holiday Cookie Co-Op   Save yourself the time, money, and energy of baking various types of cookies by having a cookie co-op. Here's how it works.

People are invited to come to a home and bring a certain type of holiday treat or cookie. Batches must be large enough for each person to receive a minimum of a dozen cookies from each platter.

Tell each person to bring a large cookie platter to fill.

Place all the cookie platters on a dining table and form an assembly line, taking cookies of each type to make a platter.

Serve coffee and tea to go with samples after the platters are assembled. You can take advantage of the gathering for informal sharing and prayer in the spirit of the season.

Christmas Party/Progressive Dinner

Energizing and financing a Christmas party ask a great deal of the hostess. Instead of knocking holes in your head and purse, share the load and make it interesting.

- Form a nucleus of three couples to host a Christmas party/progressive dinner.
- Assign appetizers, dinner, and dessert to each couple.
- Send out invitations instructing friends that the party will begin at "The Appetizers" and progress accordingly.

Midnight Munch

Hosting a New Year's Eve party can be a long evening since the reason people come revolves around what happens at midnight. To conserve finances and energy, start later.

Start your party after the dinner hour, around 8:00 P.M. Serve snacks and desserts. Make it light fare, and focus mainly on entertainment. Ask guests to bring a dessert or snack, and you supply the drinks and coffee.

When midnight rolls around, celebrate meaningfully.

- Share New Year's resolutions or dreams for the coming year.
- Have a praise and prayer celebration. Select Bible passages that speak of commitments, and talk and pray about new beginnings.

22 • Lunches that Work for Working People

A common dilemma for budget-conscious people concerns the amount of money spent on going out to lunch with coworkers. Usually, one can plan on spending a minimum of $3 to $5 and up to $10 for this habit. Simple math tells us that means $15 to $25 per week, $60 to $100 per month, and $720 to $1,200 per year. What could you do with $700 to $1,200?

On the other side of the coin, the common excuse is time. In our fast-paced culture, moms, dads, and singles maintain full schedules that preclude brown-bagging it. Even if they make it to the market to stock up on fixings, sometimes they just get too busy to put the lunches together each morning. A couple working full-time can't afford *not* to take lunches on most days, however.

"What Can I Make?"

Prepare lunches that can be made quickly and complemented with a snack or fruit. The key factor is preparing something you can use for two to three days before switching to something else or having to go to the store again. Along these lines, the following dishes work well:

- Chicken salad
- Tuna or tuna salad
- Sunday roast, ham, or turkey
- Pasta salad
- Spaghetti
- Lasagna

"When Do I Prepare These Dishes?"

Sunday evening is the best time to get ready for the week. Assuming you have the ingredients, you need a couple of hours after dinner. You could slice leftover ham or roast for the week or make a bowl of tuna.

This time is well invested because it cuts down on the time required in the morning to make lunch. Best of all, you save the expense of eating out. Perhaps you can treat yourself to a lunch out once a month as a reward.

23 • For Nonfrequent Flyers

Air travel has become increasingly attractive since major carriers started offering a variety of perks for customers exclusively choosing their airline.

The only problem is that there are more nonfrequent flyers in America than frequent flyers. These folks don't log enough miles for free companion tickets and other benefits. When it is time to see your grandchildren, flock to a family reunion, or just go home, don't despair. Diligence and/or patience will secure you a special fare.

Advance Purchase   The general rule of thumb is to make your reservation far ahead of time to get a low fare. The only (and significant) danger with advance purchases is that they carry stiff penalties and restrictions. Usually, any change will cost you the price of your ticket. But if your health is good and the occasion is a reasonably safe bet, this is the easiest and most expedient way to save on your airfare.

A Time for Peace and a Time for "Air Wars"   The airline industry has been very reactionary since it was deregulated. This development has good and bad effects for the consumer. On the one hand, carriers are free to hold a mobile society hostage with high prices. On the other hand, economic downturns, real or perceived, spark regional, national, and international price wars. Fortunately for consumers, America has so many economic indexes that can set these skirmishes off that it's usually a yearly phenomenon. In some regions of the country it's so competitive that fares are low year-round.

Travel Agent Who Will Work for You

When one couple lived in Dallas, their homecomings were in California. Their travel agent knew that their budget was limited and that they needed help. Because of her diligence, they were able to purchase individual $165 round-trip airfares. To get this fare, she set up two separate round trips per person, connecting in Phoenix. If you are willing to make the connections, you will save. You may have to recheck luggage as well, but it's a small price to pay for big savings. If you can't find a good travel agent, get a flight guide and make the arrangements yourself.

If Time Is on Your Side

This savings tip is for ticketed passengers en route. When a flight is overbooked, interested travelers are given an opportunity to give up their seats (be bumped) in return for vouchers worth hundreds in air travel. If time is on your side, you can make easy money.

24 • Saving on Wedding Gifts

Perhaps you've been faced with a situation similar to that of a young couple. Within a twelve-month span, seven pairs of friends walked down the aisle. Confronted with all of the weddings and a tight budget, they were in a quandary about how to buy gifts for their friends. They stumbled into a solution they adopted as a savings strategy.

While shopping at a discount club, they spotted a stylish thermos for serving coffee. They put it in their cart because they needed one. Then it hit them. The thermos was a gift perfect for newly-weds, and it was discounted $10.

They bought several, and without exception, each couple commented about the gift's usefulness. It's great when you find a winner. In that instance, it solved two major problems associated with buying wedding gifts. First, it saved the couple from making several shopping trips. Second, it kept them from paying top dollar associated with last-minute impulse shopping.

Stick with a Winner   When you know you will be attending a few weddings or will have occasion to attend a shower this year, you will save money by finding and sticking with a winner gift.

- When shopping for your next wedding, look for a gift on sale that would be practical for most couples. A coffee thermos isn't a bad start unless you're buying the gift for a close relative.
- When you find the right gift on sale, buy two or three for weddings to come. If you have a large family or large circle of friends, you shouldn't hesitate.
- Save the receipt just in case you want to return one later.

25 • Financial Cholesterol

Hardening of the arteries is a condition that involves a thickening and hardening of the arterial walls over time. If unchecked, it can kill a person. The solution for people with this condition is to change their eating and exercise habits. More specifically, they have to cut out foods high in cholesterol.

Many family spending plans are experiencing a budgetary hardening of the arteries. They have become accustomed to a number of items or luxuries they could effectively do without and save a great deal of money. In this instance, cutting out the fat and exercising self-discipline and creativity in spending will improve financial health.

Trim the Fat Trimming excesses from spending requires introspection and honesty with regard to needs versus wants and what's best over the long term. Ask yourself, How would my life change if I eliminated completely some of the following things? How would it change if I less frequently indulged in them? How would I benefit personally? How would my family benefit? How would my spending plan benefit?

- Magazine subscriptions
- Car washes
- Baby-sitters
- Excessive recreational spending
- Buying on credit
- Need-driven shopping instead of planned shopping with coupons and at sales
- Eating out
- Impulse buying of personal items
- Long-distance calls
- Entertainment
- Vacations

Seek Balance   There is a balance that allows for freedom and an imbalance that places you in financial bondage. An effective way to stretch your hard-earned money is to cut out unnecessary expenses.

26 • Letting the "Air" Out of High-Priced Tennis Shoes

It is a ritual that has deep roots in our lives. Whether we were starting our first day of school, made the basketball team, or bought our first suit, we needed a new pair of shoes to go with our station in life. Some styles were more "in" than others, and we had to look our part. Sneakers, Buster Browns, wing tips, penny loafers, pumps, platform heels, waffle stompers, earth shoes, flip-flops, ropers, saddle shoes, and other makes tickled our feet.

Even though we are older, more mature, self-confident, and secure, it seems that we haven't lost our fixation with shoes—especially tennis shoes.

With tennis shoes taking over center stage in our culture, retailers charge premium prices for popular styles, some going over the $100 mark. And for families with teenagers and adults going through this culture phase where identity is intimately connected to our feet, we have to think on our feet to find bargains. Here are some pointers from a tennis shoe bargain hunter.

Tennis Shoe Cents   Larger inventories mean lower prices. They also mean retailers with big supplies must keep volume up and have more freedom to deal.

- *Don't* buy tennis shoes at retail mall stores unless they are going out of business. They rarely offer more than a 10 percent discount on their shoes. You can get a better deal on the same shoe elsewhere.
- Buy from large sporting good chains, factory outlets, and tennis shoe wholesalers. These merchants can offer you 25 to 40 percent off retail by carrying larger inventories. They usually have wider selections as well.
- Visit discount clothing stores. Stores such as Marshalls, Ross, and T J Maxx often get shipments of high-quality shoes and sell them at 40 to 60 percent off.
- If you have access to a discount or wholesale club, check the shoe section for recent shipments of tennis shoes. You will have to catch them at the right time since "hot" items at low prices sell fast.

To find these sporting goods chains, outlets, and wholesale stores, resource your Yellow Pages under "sporting goods" or "shoes." If you know of an outlet mall near you, call ahead to find out if an athletic store is represented.

27 • Cashing In on Car Repair

Most Americans place car repair in the same category as their mortgage—at least they do when they have to pay. The feeling is that you can't function without wheels just as you can't live without a roof over your head. You just don't think about it, so you pay it. The difference is that a house has fewer moving parts, which minimizes the chances of its ceasing to function.

The Car Repair Credo

> Savings on car repair and maintenance costs can be greatly increased when a conscientious program of care is implemented.

We should treat our cars the way we are advised to treat our mouths. Conscientiously maintain our cars to avoid big problems and bills. Major problems with a car usually are not the result of recklessly driving it into the ground on a particular day. Like most major problems in life in which we play a part, they are results of little choices *not* to do what we needed to do. These small compromises, lapses, decisions, rationalizations, or whatever you want to call them snowball and eventually bring consequences.

How to Avoid Car Surgery and Save Money   You can make a choice today to save on car repair by acting on one of the following suggestions.

1. *Take a simple course on basic auto maintenance and repair.* Call a local vocational-technical school, junior college, high school, or community center to inquire about where these courses are offered.

The short-term investment of tuition and time will yield dividends on car repairs the rest of your life. You will learn how to

- check the oil level.
- add oil.
- change the oil and filter.
- check the transmission fluid level.
- add transmission fluid.
- check/add brake fluid.
- check/add antifreeze.
- check/replace the air filter.
- install a battery.
- replace fuses.
- check air pressure.
- change tires.
- do a tune-up.

Doing basic maintenance yourself is the absolute best way to save. Your labor is free. You can save hundreds in service and tune-up costs. Take a class with a friend.

2. If you are not servicing your own car, *find a qualified mechanic* and have him outline a program of maintenance for your car. If you haven't followed your manual's recommended schedule, he can put you on track. Survey acquaintances, family, or friends to locate a mechanic you can trust.

3. For major car repairs, *compare prices* with your mechanic, dealers, and specialty car care centers (brakes, mufflers, transmissions, etc.) and find the lowest cost. You may want to check around to be sure that the place you choose has a record of reliability and trustworthiness.

28 • Clutter Cash

Clutter. It means something different for every family. For some, it's Dad's fishing gear in the garage. For others, it's the stuff in the hall closet. And for others, it's whatever is lurking in the shack in the backyard. Everyone has clutter.

One family with seven children would have won the clutter award on the block judging from all the items in the garage: desks, luggage, surfboards, fishing poles, clothes, dressers, sporting equipment, record albums, Tupperware, and miscellany spanning two decades of growth. Big family, big clutter.

There's Clout in Clutter Instead of throwing it away, turn clutter into cash. Spring cleaning can be spring cleanup. Many families can benefit financially through clutter management.

Whether it's spring cleaning time or you are moving, take advantage of any opportunity to purge your garage and earn some cash.

Have a Garage Sale

Believe it or not, there is a large and active market for that rusty bike and old desk. Pick a weekend, buy a classified ad, put up some signs, and get ready. You will be surprised at what people will pay for your throwaways.

Put It on Consignment

If you don't want to energize a garage sale, look up your local consignment store and find out if it will sell what you have. Your stuff will receive a better venue and be regularly exposed to buyers.

Get a Tax Deduction

Gather up your clutter, give it to a charitable organization (Salvation Army, Goodwill, etc.), and get a receipt. List the items on your next tax return. If you contribute items worth $150, you can save $30 to $50 on your taxes.

It is possible to give new life to your clutter. Pass it on to others and receive cash for it.

29 • Fun Furnishings for Kids

Have you ever been in a home and seen a piece that looked like a million bucks only to learn that it was just a junker before someone discovered it? Such pieces are the most admired furnishings in a home. They can share the same room with more expensive pieces, but it doesn't seem to matter. The difference is that one piece has a story to tell, and the others don't.

Furnishing children's rooms with personal projects need not be a strenuous or expensive venture. You can use flea market finds, consignment catches, and garage sale gimmies to work your magic.

Plan Your Creation   Invite a friend to join you in this venture, and follow this plan.

Find the piece you need. Check the newspaper for garage sales as well as nearby consignment shops.

Once you have found your piece, purchase your materials and set up a work area. You will need the following:

- Stencils. Check with a local arts/crafts store or make your own.

- Paint. You will need white primer paint as well as primary colors. Check with the store about whether you should use can or spray paint.
- Dropcloth and/or cardboard. It will keep you from painting the ground.
- Masking tape. Use it for making borders and when putting multiple colors on one piece.

Lightly sand the piece so it will receive the paint.

Apply primer coats and then your primary colors. Do any detailed work to finish the piece.

Stand back and admire your work of art.

30 • What to Cook When You're Expecting

On one flight a man shared that he and his wife were expecting their first child. During the two- to three-month period of adjustment after the baby is born, every parent will be tested by the level of attention a newborn needs and by how physically and emotionally draining it can be. New families order out a lot after the delivery of a baby. Mom is simply not going to be able to stand on her feet much, and depending on the relative ease or complexity of delivery, this time period can vary dramatically. And Dad is probably working during the day and then coming home to help Mom with the baby.

This father-to-be and his spouse had worked out a plan for meals after they had their baby. Their forethought on how to reduce expenses for food is admirable.

How to Go About It   Two weeks before the due date, this couple drew up a list of meals to precook and freeze. These meals would be used specifically for the time after the baby was born. Frozen vegetables could be added, so very little actual preparation would be necessary.

Some planning in this area with children, friends, and families could mean significant dollars staying in purses or going to the baby's gift fund. The plan is as follows:

- Make a list of dishes in your mealtime repertoire that are easy to fix and keep well. Examples are spaghetti sauce, stew, soups, and sloppy joe filling.
- One week prior to the due date, set aside two evenings to cook.
- Go to the market for ingredients (better yet —send your spouse with a complete marketing list and coupons).
- Invite your relatives and friends over. Make an event out of it.
- Have meal preparation instructions handy, and give out the assignments.
- Store and freeze your meals until after the baby comes and have proud Papa and friends prepare the meals.

Estimated Savings   Feeding two adults from take-out costs a minimum of $5 to $8 and can get as high as $20 with drinks. Savings for a three-week period could be as much as $300. So if you or someone you love is expecting a new arrival soon, plan ahead.

31 • ATM: Always Teasing Me

ATMs (automated teller machines) are deceptive. It's too easy to get money and just as easy, or easier, to spend it. The ATM doesn't warn us, for instance, "Are you sure you need that much?" It lets us get what we want when we want it. One side of us likes that it's painless, and then the other side turns the light of conscience on. We see which side won the battle around tax time when large portions of our income are unaccounted for.

Always Taking Money   ATMs can cause problems for you for several reasons:

- They are too convenient.
- They exploit a natural lack of discipline.
- They don't ask questions.
- They don't tell you your balance in lieu of uncleared checks.
- They facilitate impulse buying.
- They don't register what you spend the money on.
- They assess transaction fees for ATM with-

drawals at locations other than your own bank.

Avoid Teller Mania These suggestions may help you in this area:

- Set a limit to the amount you withdraw.
- Keep the receipt and track the spending of the amount withdrawn on the back.
- Leave your card at home. Get a preset amount of cash for time between pay periods that is appropriate for your budget.
- Withdraw money only at branch offices of your bank to save transaction charges.
- Leave your card at home to avoid impulsive use and buying.
- Never withdraw funds based on a balance other than the one in your checkbook.

32 • Christmas in October

The kids are back at school. Football season is in full swing. The leaves are turning their seasonal reds and oranges. The air is a little cooler. The sun goes down earlier. Dad's gotta mulch the lawn. Oh, yeah, don't forget the kids get out of school on Columbus Day. Tick tock, ho-hum, and on rolls the month of October in the United States.

It's certainly life at its own speed except in one place—the mall. You see, merchants have a problem with the month of October. There are no holiday or behavior cycles absolutely requiring people to spend money. Their solution for this traditionally slow month is to create special sales. These sales are for sales' sake.

October is a window for relaxed Christmas shopping with big savings as the dividend. Admittedly, motivating yourself may require a little adjustment in your holiday routine, especially if you are a traditional after-Thanksgiving shopper. But time and savings factors should help you make the switch. If you're still not convinced, consider the Black Friday Syndrome.

The day after Thanksgiving, Americans search

for "the deals." The result is a shopper's nightmare of long lines at cash registers, parking problems, and picked-over merchandise.

Bargains, short lines, plenty of parking, good selections, and longer sales periods sound tempting, don't they? If you are going to make the switch, here's the plan.

The Official "I Want to Save Time and Money and Be Emotionally Healthy for the Holidays" Plan for October Shopping   Make a note in the calendar you use today. Enter the following message on October 1: "Christmas gift sales."

When October arrives, start asking family members questions about needs and wants. Listen for clues and write down what you hear.

Put your sales radar on. Watch for advertisements on TV and in the newspaper. They will be hard to miss.

Take advantage of openings in your schedule to shop. Make the sacrifice now, and you'll thank yourself when you see the poor unfortunate souls who go off to combat duty on the day after Thanksgiving.

Save all your receipts and keep them accessible. You may need to make an exchange or last-second return. (Keep checking the current price of the merchandise you purchase; some stores will reimburse you if they lower the price of the items you purchased.)

33 • Circular Reasoning

The glossy and colored ink inserts in the newspaper are known as circulars. They are used primarily by grocery stores, drugstores, department stores, and appliance stores to highlight sales and specials. They represent the ongoing battle for customers between the drugstores and grocery chains and between major department store chains.

They enable you to compare prices on everyday items (grocery and drug circulars) and give you a sense of where the savings are on retail goods (department store circulars). The bottom line is savings on things the family needs—whether diapers or hairspray or a video camera. Here is the best way for taking advantage of the circulars.

Grocery-Drugstore Comparison   Read through the grocery and drugstore circulars noting items on your marketing list and their prices at the different stores. Compare prices and make a list of the items you will purchase at each store.

Look for patterns of savings. After a while you

will know instinctively, for example, that Drug-store A is the place to buy diapers.

Date: _____

Grocery-Drugstore Comparison

Item	Grocery A Price	Grocery B Price	Drugstore A Price	Drugstore B Price
1. Huggies	$9.98	$8.75	$9.00	$9.50
2.				
3.				
4.				
5.				
6.				
7.				
8.				
9.				
10.				
11.				
12.				

Department Store Comparison

Similarly, make your list of items you are shopping for at the department store: clothes, electronics, tools, and so on. Read over the department store circulars and compare prices on similar items. Make a list of the items you will purchase at each store.

Look for patterns of savings on different categories of merchandise. Eventually, one of these stores will be the place to go for gardening tools or sports equipment or whatever.

Date: _____

Department Store Comparison

Item	Sears	J. C. Penney	M. Ward
Camcorder	$799.00	$725.00	$674.00
Bath towels	$ 4.99	$ 6.99	$ 5.99

34 • There's Power in Numbers

It's no secret that larger inventories (greater volume of goods) mean a lower unit cost per item. And until recent years, the average consumer was unable to bypass the middleman and go straight to the wholesaler. Today, however, a number of wholesale clubs offer substantial discounts for individuals buying in bulk.

A common problem is that you can't buy just one item. You have to buy five or more. So you might walk out with lots of toothpaste and toilet paper, but that is about it.

One way to sidestep this problem is to adopt the same principle of these warehouses: increase your numbers; lower your price. Practically, that means joining two or three families to perform group buys. You can get the items you need at the prices you want without being stuck with a gross of one item.

Getting the Sale from Wholesalers

Secure a membership. Although different warehouses have varying requirements, they are fairly easy to obtain. Some are free; others require a business sponsorship. If that is your case, consider asking your employer to sponsor a card for you, or start a simple at-home business that can serve friends locally or commercially. (Don't let this prospect scare you off. One woman started a little decorating business on the side making arrangements for friends, and she signed up two other families on her card. After learning on her own, she now owns and operates a franchise of a decorating chain.)

Invite families to participate in a group buying network. To do this, they must know what items are offered. You may want to do a walk-through. After you've determined what items are available and are in common, decide on a quantity that can be evenly and periodically dispersed.

Assign a regular time line to your buys—once a month, every other month. Your time line should reflect usage over time of the particular items bought.

Rotate responsibility for people making the buys.

Keep receipts and reimburse or give the cash up front to the designated buyer for the period. You must set up a system for reimbursement/collection of funds that is easy for the buyer.

Compare wholesale prices with your local grocery store. Some items offer substantial savings for the consumer, but others afford little or no savings.

35 • Beyond Coupons to Refunds

Taking advantage of refund offers is similar to using coupons but requires a little more effort and organization. The benefit is that you can save hundreds of dollars in cash, manufacturers' coupons, and merchandise received. You *make money* by getting cash back on products you have already purchased and would have purchased regardless of the refund offer.

Where Can You Find Refund Offers?

Look in the newspaper. Keep your eyes open in the store. When you go shopping, take a quick walk up and down all aisles. Manufacturers often display refund offers on the shelves containing their products. Some stores have a board where they display all available refund offers. Other sources include direct mail, magazines, and specially marked packages. Go through your cabinets, and you'll be surprised how many canned goods have refund offers inside the labels. Look for "Details inside" on the label.

Save all refund offers you come across. They are usually good for a couple of months, and you may need or want the product in that period of time.

How Do Refund Offers Work?   Refund
offers usually require you to send in various proofs of your purchases: proof of purchase seals found on product packaging, the universal product code (UPC code), and virtually anything on the product packaging.

Before you throw away or recycle a product package, remove the proof of purchase. Or you may want to save the entire package. You never know when a great refund offer will come your way. Store these packages in a box or envelopes.

Keep all of your grocery receipts. Some refund offers also require you to send the cash register receipt with the price paid for the product circled.

Organize Your Refund Offers   Set
aside thirty minutes a week to organize your refund offers. Gather the requirements for the offers, file proofs of purchase and receipts, and send in the offers for your refund. To make the process easier, design a refund form to use when gathering information on refunds. Design your form on a computer and print several copies, or do it by hand and make several photocopies.

Sample Refund Form

Expiration Date: _____

Offer: _____

Requirements: _____

Address: _____

Date Sent: _____

Date Refund Expected: _____

Refund Arrived?   Yes ☐

No ☐ Action Taken: _____

Total Savings: _____

This form will help you prepare to send in the refund. Use one form per refund offer, and then file the forms by expiration date in a binder.

Have your refund binder handy when you plan your menus for the week and make your marketing list. Take it to the market with you for easy reference when making decisions on product purchases.

If your refund hasn't arrived after twelve weeks, contact the corporate headquarters of the company offering the refund and explain your situation. The address is probably on the product package.

Get on Mailing Lists   By responding to refunds, you will become a part of the company's mailing list, which can lead to even more savings.

You will most likely receive product samples, coupons, and more refund offers.

Refunding at Work   The ideal situation is to find the product you like on sale, use a double coupon when purchasing it, and send in for a refund. Here's refunding at its best:

Tide (on sale)	[$3.49]
$0.50 coupon— doubled	$1.00
Refund offer	$3.49
Postage	[$0.29]
Total savings	In this case, the Tide was free, and the profit was $0.71.

Diapers at regular price	$10.99
Diapers on sale	[$9.99]
$1.00 coupon— doubled	$7.99
$1.00 refund	$6.99
Postage	[$0.29]
Total price paid for diapers after refund	$7.28
Total savings	$3.71

A scenario like this once a month would result in a savings of about $45 a year!

36 • Entertainment, Growth, and Development

One of the best deals for entertainment, social development, and personal growth goes largely unnoticed and unused by most Americans. Most of us opt for the highly visible, media-endorsed modes of spending our spare time. But it's time we invest our lives in those things that deepen our appreciation for life, for others, and for the special talents God has bestowed on each of us. And it won't cost us a penny.

America's churches, though not perfect, offer experiences and encounters that meet practical and emotional needs.

Plug into the Church

For Your Benefit

In addition to Bible study and educational classes, your church may offer the following:

- Recreation activities
- Singles groups
- Married groups
- Family workshops

- Expectant mothers groups
- Divorce recovery groups
- College groups
- Support for persons with cancer
- Blended families groups
- Single parents groups

For Benefit of Others

Various ministries are available:

- Choir ministry
- Music ministry
- Child-care ministry
- Greeting ministry
- Feeding the poor
- Drama ministry
- Missions
- Prison ministry
- Nursing home visitation program

For Benefit of the Community

Corporate worship contributes positively to the life and health of a community.

37 • Family Slumber Party

A sure way to make a memory with kids is to have the grown-ups do something kids enjoy. If that is true, we need to ask ourselves, What do kids get excited about? Recall yourself as a child under the age of twelve and then answer. I can think of a few things I got excited about. One was being able to stay up way past my bedtime with the "older people." A second thing was the unrestrained eating of sweets.

Well, parents, if the ever-increasing costs of entertainment are bothersome and you can handle a little controlled anarchy, it's time to throw the Family Slumber Party.

The Revolution Has Begun   Explain to the family that there is going to be a slumber party on a given night and that you need their help planning it. Poll family members about what they want to eat, games they want to play, movies they want to watch, and so on. Give them ownership of the planning. Assign different areas to family members to make the choice.

Lay down the rules:

- Everyone is in pj's.
- Everyone sleeps in the living room (or family room).
- No bedtime will be assigned.
- Pillow fights must abide by certain guidelines.

Plan a simple dinner (hot dogs, pizza, etc.) and a specific time for everyone to be in the living room to start the evening activities. No starting the party until everyone is in pj's.

Clear a large space in the living room, and fill it with pillows, comforters, and sleeping bags.

For breakfast, make the traditional "slumber cakes" (pancakes) to top off the party in true style.

Schedule

7:00 P.M.	Dinner
7:45	Everyone in pj's; dessert
8:30	Board games
9:30	King of the Hill with pillows
10:00	Cocoa break; start video

The Family Slumber Party is quality time without the expense. Be sure to take pictures of this out-of-the-ordinary evening. The kids will love to see pictures of the night when they had the run of the house!

38 • Bravo! An Encore of Savings

A regular helping of the theater is out of the question for a great many aficionados. For them, the season may represent one or possibly two performances because of ticket prices.

Feeling the Pinch?   If you are romantically drawn to the theater but financially question the relationship this season, consider sacrificing a little ambience of evening performances and traditions to see the productions.

Recently, a close friend explained how she takes advantage of matinee performances. She has traded the nightlife of theatrical events for significant savings on ticket prices and attendance at productions she has an interest in. And although the stylish dress and dinners may be missing, matinee performances can be special, too.

A Midsummer Afternoon's Dream
Plan the purchase of your tickets. Do your homework to determine how far in advance you will need to buy your seat(s). Call the theater for its schedule and ticket information. Put the date in

your calendar, and save or set aside the money so that you are ready to purchase the tickets when they go on sale.

Plan a special lunch. It could even be a picnic in the park prior to the performance. Perhaps you can bring the sound track and play it while you picnic to prime yourself for the production. Whatever you choose to do, toast the occasion in your own special way.

Purchase your tickets on the day noted in your calendar.

Clear your schedule, and make necessary arrangements (at work, with the family) to attend the showing.

Get ready for Act 1, Scene 1!

39 • Solution to the Budget Blues

Are you in control of your money, or is your money controlling you?

A common illusion is that if you make more money, there will be less worry. Intellectually, that is what many people believe, but practically, the opposite experience is true. It becomes increasingly difficult to know exactly how much you have and where it goes. It is especially troublesome when you have to make any financial commitment.

Unfortunately, people take on new financial commitments without seeing the exact numbers and base their decision on a "sense" or "feeling." Suddenly, they find themselves overbudgeted and anxious, saying to themselves, "How in the world did this happen?" That is why you need to have your income and all your expenses clearly laid out before you prior to making any large financial commitment. One way to keep yourself from spending funds you don't have is to computerize your spending plan. Anything that helps you gain control of finances inevitably helps you save money.

The Benefits of Computerizing Your Spending Plan   With computers and computer software readily available and competitively priced, families should make this investment. Not only will it save you time when you have to pay the bills, but it will help you gain control of your money, which will save you some bucks.

Here are some ways computers can help.

- Organizes your expenses into categories for your utilities, clothes, and so on, and tracks your spending in each area on a monthly basis.
- Provides spending reports. With them, you can see how well your actual spending compares with your established spending plan.
- Provides a financial statement that shows your income, expenses, and net worth.
- Provides all your itemized deductions at tax time.

40 • Family Savings and Giving Project

One young couple operating on a limited budget the first year of marriage had to forgo many seasonal holidays with family because of the distance separating them. Round-trip airfares for two were simply too expensive.

One year the father-in-law called and asked about Christmas plans. The husband informed him that the spirit was willing but the wallet was weak. Being a talented business consultant and never at a loss for ideas, Dad said that they were going to start a Christmas fund for the couple. He explained that they were going to place a jug in the kitchen and drop loose change and bills in there to cover the costs of airfare.

What happened was phenomenal. The whole family got into it, and so did many others. Visiting friends started putting $5 and $10 in the jug. Repairmen fixing appliances at the house would inquire and contribute. As Christmas got closer, Dad told the couple to book the flights because it looked like the jug would be filled. When the couple counted the money, they were amazed that the amount raised was within several dollars of the total needed.

Putting Lost Dollars to Work   You

know how it works. You go to your bank or ATM and get cash for the week. Pretty soon one ten or twenty is running into another, one endless seam of spending with no beginning or end. One transaction runs into another; you run low on cash; you get more and continue the cycle. And although you may remember the reasons behind the withdrawals, you usually take more than you need and end up cycling the balance to what I call the amoeba spending program. This program has no shape or form. Loose bills and change just float out of your purse and wallet somewhere, but no one knows where "somewhere" is. It's money in orbit. What follows is a plan for putting the lost dollars to work.

The true purpose of this plan is to fund something meaningful to you. It could be bringing a college student home for a holiday or supporting a needy child in the Third World. If it is to be successful, you need to make your effort as personal as possible. It's a great way to start turning cups of coffee, candy bars, and magazines from the checkout line into a significant investment.

Jug Project   Poll your spouse and family to

determine what they would like the project to accomplish. You may already have an idea in mind. Just make sure the goal is proportional to the size of the jug. (Also, have a realistic time line for accomplishing your goal. If you want to take a summer vacation, start dropping coins in the jug in the fall.)

Explain how the family is to make deposits into the jug on a daily basis:

- Check pockets and wallets during the day.
- Make contributions instead of buying something for yourself.
- Do some extra work and put the money toward the project.
- Every time you break $20, tuck away $1 for your fund.

Find a clear jug or large jar (one you can easily retrieve the money from), label it, and place it in the kitchen or an otherwise highly visible location for the family. Seal the jar with masking tape so no one will be tempted to remove some emergency cash.

Make an initial contribution to kick off the project. Empty out your penny cup or change jar, and add a few bills to start.

Occasionally, you may want to say a prayer at mealtime for the people or project for which you are saving. This helps to knit family members to the project in a special way and acknowledges the big picture regarding your efforts.

When the deadline arrives, count the funds and present them to the people or project.

41 • Shopping Outlet Malls

Factory outlet malls provide brand name retail and home furnishings at attractive discounts for consumers. You can find a wide variety of items ranging from men's and women's clothes to sportswear to china at 25 to 75 percent off retail prices. Malls can overwhelm the shopper who simply shows up for bargains without a plan of attack. Many people visiting outlet malls get frustrated by the large crowds and seemingly endless racks of merchandise. So don't go to the outlet malls and expect to window shop or leisurely browse and select the things you need. This is war!

One young mother's experience is a case in point. Accompanied by a good friend, she and her two-month-old embarked for the outlet mall at the relaxed time of 1:00 P.M. on a Saturday. Bad move. The crowds, the baby, the parking problems, and a rainstorm turned it into a "never again" experience.

She handled her next trip differently. She had control of the outlet mall; the outlet mall did not have control of her. Planning and fact finding gave her the edge as she undertook her Buying Operation for Outlet Malls (BOOM).

1. Shop outlet malls seasonally

Plan to cover all your gift giving over a two- to three-month period. It may seem like a big chunk of your budget, but you will come out on top when compared to impulse buying for each separate occasion.

2. Gather intelligence information

Just as gathering intelligence information means gaining an advantage against the enemy in warfare, the same principle applies to shopping the outlet mall. Call ahead to find what retail chains are represented. Even better is to call the stores and ask what is available.

3. Plan not to take the children

If possible, make this trip a solo venture or go with a friend. Plan to leave children with relatives or spouses for the day. Between the throngs of people and the vastness of outlet malls, little loved ones can be hard to keep tabs on.

4. Attack under cover of morning

With your battle plan and gift list in hand, make it your mission to be there when the doors open. Diminished crowds free you up to relax (a little), give you a wider selection, and save you time.

42 • Home Is Where Your Heart Is

My wife is lucky to have a mother who is skilled at making decorations for the home. Something about homemade decorations adds a certain feel to a home. People have commented to us that when they walk into our place, they feel right at home. They see oak pinwheel chairs, silk flower arrangements, colorful wreaths, lots of cozy blankets and afghans, handmade baskets, and many other personal artifacts that say to people we like to spend time in our home. Almost every decoration has a story behind it, usually one of care, family, and resourcefulness.

Your home can be warm and attractive without spending a fortune. For example, my wife always receives compliments on a beautiful basket she painted and decorated with a bow of floral cloth. To this day I have not seen a more beautiful basket, and we frequent a lot of boutiques. It cost her $20 to $25 to make, and similar baskets run from $75 to $100. So when I look at that basket, I admire its decorative qualities and also see $50 or more that we saved. The story of how the basket came into being illustrates further why interior decorating can be easy to do as well as pay dividends.

The basket would have never come into being had it not been for a family friend. She invited four women to her home and instructed them to bring a large basket and a yard of floral material. Together, they constructed the bows, painted the rims, and attached patterns to their baskets by following a plan in a crafts book. None of them had ever done that before.

Decorate Together   This little experience suggests some simple steps you can take to save money decorating your home and develop a sense of community.

- Get people together to work on a project.
- Find ideas in decorating books available at your local crafts store or the library.
- Buy materials for decorations and put them into arrangements yourself.
- If your friends show no interest, take a class yourself. Call your local crafts store and inquire about where such classes are offered. Many hold classes on the premises.

As with so many other areas, spending less and investing your efforts increase the value and quality of things.

43 • Moving Your Belongings

Anyone who has ever moved from an apartment or a house knows that the only adventurous aspect of moving is discovering just how much stuff you have accumulated and somehow making it all fit in the truck. If you are moving yourself or your family, here are some tips from a veteran of many moves.

The Truck: Just Rent It! The difference in cost between renting a truck and paying a moving company is literally thousands of dollars. Enough said. Still, make sure you compare at least three rental companies before signing on the dotted line. Depending on the length of your move and circumstances, that could mean hundreds of dollars. You can use the information you gather to bid down the other agencies.

Don't Move What You Don't Need How many times have you told yourself you are going to sell that old file cabinet or bike taking up space in the garage? If you have never had a garage sale, now is the time. From clothes to barbells the rule is, if you don't use it, don't move it.

What you don't sell can be given to charity and taken as a tax deduction. Additionally, friends could cosponsor a neighborhood garage sale. You're likely to get rid of more stuff *and* get cash for it.

Materials   Every move involves lots of boxes, tape, labels, and stuffing. Savings tips here include the following:

- Don't buy boxes unless it is absolutely necessary. The best way to get the boxes you need is to talk with the produce manager at your local grocery store and ask him to set aside boxes for you. Form-fitting apple and orange boxes are the best because they require little tape. For bigger boxes, check with local merchants or check dumpsters behind malls or grocery stores. Buying corrugated boxes from an agency can cost $100 or more.
- Buy large rolls of tape and tape dispensers at the hardware store. The smaller dispensers in grocery and convenience stores are not economical. Check to see if a friend or an employer has large packing tape dispensers you can use. They will save you a good deal of time and hassle.

Blankets   For every blanket you get from an agency you will pay to use it, and it is not for keeps. It's a lost investment. As you pack, set aside old sheets, blankets, or rugs you can use to protect furniture as you load the truck.

On the Road Again   Pack your own food.
Food from convenience stores and meals in restaurants add up on a long move. Buy your drinks, snack items, and fruit beforehand. You will stay on the road more and in the restaurants less besides saving money.

If you have to stop over, deals on hotels and motels are available in the form of coupons in road atlases or through auto clubs. Take advantage. If possible, stay with friends or relatives along the way.

Save on your gas expense by driving the speed limit. Heavy loads at high speeds cost the mover.

44 • Saving on Seasons Greetings

Every Christmas, families receive beautiful cards. Each one has its own message and magic. Images of the season, messages of joy, nativity scenes, and other meaningful symbols of Christmas carry the special signature of the person who sent the card. Out of all the cards to choose from, the person selected just one.

Perhaps you hang onto them for months before you throw them away. What else can you do with used Christmas cards?

Showcase and Save   Instead of putting these cards into the junk drawer, dresser, or mailbasket for a spell and throwing them away, give them another life. Pass the beauty and blessing of these cards on to others. You save money by buying fewer cards next year, and you do your part in our recycling-conscious culture.

- Keep a shoe box and a pair of scissors handy when cards start to arrive.
- After the family has a chance to appreciate these cards (reading them, stringing them above the fireplace, showcasing on the man-

tel, etc.), cut off the half containing the Christmas message, and save the other half.

- Place a number in pencil on the top right corner of the card and keep a log that tells who sent it. You don't want to send the same card back to a sender.
- After the holidays pass, store your shoe box of cards with other holiday decorations for next year. Before you know it, you'll be retrieving the box.
- To use these Christmas cards, simply format them like regular postcards. Fortunately, Christmas cards have a large writing space that allows room for a personal greeting.

Advantages to Recycling Christmas Cards   You save on the purchase of Christmas cards ($4 to $10 per box) and on postage costs. Check for postal requirements. You also add a special touch with your note.

45 • Movies, Money, and Memories

One of the lines used by many a persuasive child is: "But, Mom, all the kids in school————." Just fill in the blank yourself. It could be clothes, shoes, a hairstyle, language, or just about any sociological tool kids tune into on any given week. And the traditionally wise parent replies, "Well, if all the kids at school were jumping off a cliff, would you do it, too?"

A lot of times the tension between parent and child is rooted not so much in the particular issue but in the financial aspects associated with the issue. For example, a parent may not have a problem with allowing a child to drive, but paying for the insurance is prohibitive. Parents are examples of ATM machines with arms, legs, and mouths but with one significant difference: their supply of cash is *not* unlimited (a shock to most kids).

One request that parents can honor more frequently is the desire to see a particular movie at the theater. Given that the parents approve of the content and suitability, they can plan a family day sure to please the most discriminating critics and save money in the process.

Making Matinee Memories Start a tradition of going to see a matinee with your kids once every other month on a weekend. You will save from $1.00 to $2.50 on each ticket.

Prepare a premovie meal and eat it at home to cut down on expensive and nonnutritious cinema snacks. Make it a family favorite to build excitement.

Mutually agree on a movie ahead of time that the whole family will enjoy. Animated features have broad appeal for both older and younger audiences. Sometimes there may not be a family movie to see. In that case, select an alternative activity to do together.

After the show, have a family dinner before breaking out for the evening.

This concept saves you money, but more important, a shared family experience satisfies the youthful movie craving and makes memories.

46 • Before You Get Engaged

When Beth and Joel got their wedding rings appraised for insurance purposes, anyone watching them would have seen noticeable smirks on their faces. They had taken the rings to a retail jeweler at the local mall and set up the appointment with the gemologist. He inspected the rings, made notes, and handed them an appraisal slip, which was three times the amount they had paid. In essence, he was showing them what they would have paid if they had made the purchase at a retail chain store.

The Dilemma   When it finally was time to propose marriage, all of Joel's ducks were in a row except how to get the best engagement ring for the minimum amount of money. He was at a loss. Most fiancés-to-be experience the same dilemma.

Finding a Reputable Diamond Broker
Your best first stop in the hunt is to ask recently married men how they purchased the engagement ring. Although most men believe they received a deal on the diamond, wait until someone

recommends a broker. A broker buys the diamonds directly without the costs of middlemen and passes the savings along to you.

Ask him about what the process involved. Was he able to inspect the diamond? Was the broker helpful in explaining the different sizes, qualities, styles, and prices? Was the broker able to mount the diamond? Who recommended him to this broker? Has he recommended others to this broker, and were they satisfied?

Make an appointment with the broker. Indicate a price range you can afford. Never name a specific figure. By giving a range, you will be able to inspect a wider variety of diamonds and negotiate the best diamond for your money.

Before your appointment, find out the details of the diamond purchased by the person who recommended the broker to you. The information will give you some boundaries to work from. The more information you can get ahead of time, the more leverage you have when you meet. Do a little homework and learn about carat size, levels of clarity, and how they relate to price. You can do this by visiting nearby retail chains. They are happy to have you look at diamonds.

Meet with the broker at your place of work if possible or a neutral location. Once again, explain the range that you intend to spend and that you would like to see what he has to offer in this range. Be sure that you can inspect the diamonds yourself. You will be looking for level of clarity, regardless of the size you choose. Also ask questions related to mounting and the cost involved. Some brokers will throw in the ring if you buy the diamond. For appraisal purposes, request that the gold be stamped according to quality.

Ask for a business card and discuss your delivery date.

Pay for the ring upon delivery.

Although financial abilities may differ, if you're interested in saving potentially hundreds on an engagement ring, take the time to find a good broker.

47 • The *B* Word

Just mention the word *budget* and normal, well-adjusted adults begin to feel a little warm under the collar, their palms become moist, and they just can't seem to get comfortable. Traditionally, images and perceptions of budgeting that give rise to these reactions range from general ledger nightmares to a financial ball and chain. Why are they so squeamish?

A simple illustration will make the point. Positioned just right and with the proper amount of light, a toy dinosaur casts an imposing and ominous shadow striking fear into the heart of a little boy or girl. Turn on the light and the basis of the fear disappears because the toy is exposed for what it truly is: a small plastic plaything. Most couples and families who have yet to commit to a budget see only the shadow and not the true substance of how a budget works. They've yet to turn on the light.

Click. We've turned on the light. What do we see? We see a wonderful tool that gives us freedom, helps us save, and keeps us out of or helps us get out of debt. Even more, it enables us to give charitably to our churches and to agencies that help people in need. We discover a *spending plan*. That sounds much better and suggests the wise aspect of spending and handling money carefully to avoid financial bondage. And once we have experienced financial freedom, we most likely will never look back. Who wants to go back to a life of anxiety, tension, and worry? No thanks.

A Spending Plan   The good news is that most couples, individuals, and families can implement a spending plan by reducing expenditures without significantly affecting their standard of living. Here is how you can start a spending plan today.

Step 1: What are my monthly expenses?

Fixed Spending

Giving*   _____
Mortgage/rent   _____
Residence insurance   _____
Car payment   _____

Total   _____

* The author views giving to the work of the church as a fixed expense but realizes the reader may disagree.

Variable Spending

Track over a thirty-day period.

Food	_____
Debt	_____
Utilities	_____
Insurance (life, health, auto)	_____
Entertainment/recreation	_____
Clothing allowance	_____
Medical/dental	_____
Savings	_____
Miscellaneous	_____
Total	_____

Step 2: What is my available income per month?

Salary	_____
Rents	_____
Notes	_____
Dividends	_____
Income tax refunds	_____
Other	_____
Total	_____

Step 3: Compare income versus expenses to see if I am spending too much

My income   _____
Minus my expenses (fixed/
   variable)   −_____
Balance   _____

If your balance is positive, your spending plan is working, and you need to continue monitoring it closely. If your balance is negative, you need to analyze each budget area and adjust it until the balance is positive.

Ask yourself, How can I save in each of these areas? What action will it require? How can I start to make the necessary adjustments today? Whom can I tell about my decision? What is my goal for getting out of debt?

Write down answers to these questions and share them with someone who will be able to help you stay on track.

But I Just Can't   Believe me, you are not alone. Even the most difficult situations can be turned around. Just remember it won't happen overnight. Begin by making a little decision to save or cut back, stick with it, and then move to another area once you've become consistent.

48 • Car Purchasing Power

Roger is the person you want to have with you when you purchase a car. Here's what's in his mind when he goes car shopping.

Dealer's Cost   Roger finds out the dealer's cost before setting foot on a lot. As a rule, knowledge means leverage at the negotiating table. He also finds the same car with low miles in the newspaper to tell the dealer what he's competing against. The sticker cost is irrelevant. He simply refuses to pay more than 2 to 6 percent over the dealer's cost. No "talks with the manager" necessary here. The dealer will get a profit from the sale that is proper but not disproportionate to the buyer's expense.

Before venturing onto a lot, confident that your bargaining skills will land you a deal, get the dealer's cost on the make you like. If you don't, you may think you received a deal, but the salesman had the leverage in the negotiations.

Low Mileage Rental Program   You will pay a premium for that new car smell. Another car-buying strategy Roger will investigate is former rental cars with low mileage. It is an option more and more consumers are benefiting from. There are a variety of models (even imports) to choose from, and the savings are tremendous. A $21,000 Volvo, for example, was sold for $14,000 to a couple as a former rental with low mileage.

Roger Knows Best Heed Roger's advice as you seek the best deal:

- Narrow your choice to no more than four models before going near a dealer. Don't be hustled into getting a car you can't afford.
- Check to see if the models you chose are available as slightly used rentals. Call major car rental companies. Check with the dealer.
- Determine the value of your trade-in prior to going to the dealer.
- Bargain up from the dealer's cost, not from the sticker price down.
- Don't be afraid to walk out. Leave your name and number with the salesperson. You may be surprised at the response!

49 • Smart Shopping for Men

Clothes can present men with a dilemma. If you have to wear a coat and tie every day, it's easy to wear out clothes quickly. And when you need to make good impressions with customers or the boss, it's a challenge to maintain a nice wardrobe. But how do you do it without going into debt? Fortunately, there is a way to build a quality wardrobe and brag about how much you saved to your buddies.

Timing   Timing is everything when it comes to saving money on work clothes. The best time of the year to shop for work clothes is the day after Christmas. Most men's clothing departments radically reduce their prices, even on their finest items, on December 26. Inventory your wardrobe, see what you need, and hunt for deals.

Exploring   As you do your Christmas shopping, keep your eyes peeled for items you need and make notes. Explore the men's department to get a feel for what's available. If you like a particular store's brands or clothes, ask the salespeople if the items you need will be on sale. The greatest satisfaction comes from getting quality for less.

Hunting   With your list in hand, plan your clothing expedition for dawn the morning of December 26. Consider your current wardrobe, and identify your targets. The goal is to get in and out as quickly as possible, which suits most men just fine.

What to Look For   Since the goal is quality for less, here are some items to look for and purchase at a discount:

- Cotton dress shirts
- Wool slacks
- Dress loafers
- Leather belts
- Dress socks
- Ties
- Suits
- Sport coats

The higher the quality, the more durable the item will be. Look for basics you can build from and save money in the process.

Last Christmas   Last year I saved $175 on shoes, shirts, a pair of slacks, and ties.

Item	Regular Price	Price Paid	Savings
Loafers	$120	$ 50	$ 70
2 100% cotton dress shirts (@ $38 each)	$ 76	$ 42	$ 34
Worsted wool dress slacks	$ 89	$ 48	$ 41
2 silk ties (@ $30 each)	$ 60	$ 30	$ 30
Total	$345	$170	$175

Although $170 may seem like too much to spend on one trip, it is the only trip for business clothing I will make all year. Divide the amount by twelve, and it comes out to less than $15 per month.

P.S. Women can apply this same strategy.

50 • Is Your Child College Bound?

Students who are college bound fall into two different categories: scholarshipped and nonscholarshipped. For the nonscholarshipped students and their families, many sacrifices have been made to make the reality of a college education happen. And because the money invested over four to six years will amount to tens of thousands of dollars, parents must be involved closely in the college selection process. Their involvement could save substantial amounts of money. If financing your child's college education is of concern to you, the one issue you must investigate is whether you will send him or her to a public or private institution.

Going Public Families who fall within the lower- to upper-middle-class category should strongly consider sending their child to a highly rated public institution. More than 75 percent of the nation's college students attend public institutions. And while there are several reasons for this trend, the most obvious incentive is cost. Soaring tuition costs and increasingly limited access to federal student aid are forcing parents to take a closer look at quality state schools, and they are liking what they see. Here's why.

Cost

- At most public universities, students pay less than 30 percent of the total cost of their education because the balance is subsidized through state programs.
- The average cost differential to attend one year at a public versus private university is more than $7,000.

Degree Programs Offered

- Because state schools have larger student populations, by necessity they offer a broader range of disciplines and emphases.
- State universities specialize in areas generally unavailable at private institutions (e.g., polytechnical, agriculture, or food management).
- State universities also emphasize core disciplines of engineering, business, and computer science. These fields represent higher starting salary potential upon entry into the job market.

Changing Perceptions   Public universities are benefiting from a noticeable shift in the way they are perceived academically. This trend affords a student the economic and educational benefits as well as a name looked upon favorably in the marketplace. The following eight institutions have been deemed "public Ivy Leaguers" because they compete well with their better-known counterparts.

- University of California system with Berkeley and UCLA as the flagship campuses
- Miami University of Ohio
- University of Michigan at Ann Arbor
- University of North Carolina at Chapel Hill
- University of Texas at Austin
- University of Vermont at Burlington
- University of Virginia at Charlottesville
- William and Mary College of Virginia

The best of the rest include these:

- University of Colorado at Boulder
- Georgia Institute of Technology
- New College of the University of Southern Florida
- University of Illinois at Urbana/Champaign
- Pennsylvania State University
- State University of New York at Binghamton
- University of Wisconsin at Madison

Some Suggestions   Because the quality of public schools can vary significantly from school to school, parents and the student should evaluate and apply to a qualified group of schools. Generally accepted criteria for evaluating a school are these:

- student to faculty ratios
- percentage of faculty members holding doctorates
- average classroom hours and size of classes
- number of graduate programs offered

The best evaluation a student can receive, however, is from a student attending the particular school of interest. Ask about:

- getting into requested classes
- percentage of classes taught by full professors versus graduate students
- size of classes
- interaction with faculty

51 • Reality-Based Spending

The other day Anne and Todd were exchanging baby clothes at a store. When they transacted the exchange at the register, they needed to pay a few extra dollars. As naturally as could be, Anne said, "I'll just put this on the credit card." Todd couldn't believe his eyes, and his face showed it. His brain was spinning so fast it was hard to get out his reply: "Why?" She said that she enjoyed handing over plastic much more than surrendering the dollars in her wallet.

This little story illustrates why so many Americans are totally paralyzed by a one-ounce piece of plastic. It's painless. The emotional weight of the transaction is brokered out by a mediator. The only problem is that the momentary freedom from the pain of handing over hard-earned cash pays unwelcome dividends at the end of the month. Husbands and wives are faced with the consequences of their choices, which often lead to disputes and despair.

Shop Only with Cash or Checks   One of the quickest ways to stop accruing credit card debt and get it under control is to shop only with cash or checks. I call this reality-based shopping. The motto here is: "You don't get it if you don't got it." It's living within your means, not living an illusion.

Cashing in on Savings   When you shop with plastic, you will buy more expensive items. There is a very simple reason: people who use credit cards excessively do not feel the emotional realities of the transactions. Credit cards are no-vocaine for debt. A person's finances are being drilled, but the nerves are dead.

Shopping on a cash basis or with checks forces you to feel the real emotional side of spending your hard-earned money. It forces you to deal with what's real and, consequently, to look for real deals!

52 • Turn About Is Fair Play

Many would-be, first-time home buyers are eager to take advantage of a favorable real estate situation, need the space of a home, or are sick of renting. However, they feel the situation is hopeless. Two common problems keeping them from the American dream are low savings and credit concerns, or they are burdened with some major expense they can't get rid of (medical, educational, or otherwise). Fortunately, potential home buyers caught in this tug-of-war have some options. There are ways for couples and families to get into a new home and save money.

Stretching Your Home Buying Dollar

Low-Cost Federal or State Loan

In addition to FHA loans, a new federal program called the 3/2 option is available to home buyers with little cash for a down payment. It allows for a relative, employer, or nonprofit organization to give or lend a family 2 percent of the down payment while the buyer supplies 3 percent and gets a 95 percent mortgage. The loans are offered through the Federal National Mortgage Association, or Fanny Mae.

Similarly, many states offer home buying assistance programs for residents. These programs offer mortgages at the standard commercial rate but require a minimal down payment around 5 percent. Call or write the department of housing in your state to see if you qualify.

Purchase an Owner-Financed Home

Owners in a hurry to sell may be willing to finance your purchase themselves. This strategy works well with sellers who have paid up their mortgages. In this case, the buyer pays monthly installments to the seller, and the seller transfers the title to the buyer. The seller essentially plays the role of the bank by assuming the risk.

Corporations Reselling Employee Homes

When employees transferred to new locations have difficulty selling their homes, many times they opt to sell it to their company who then needs to unload the property. Houses owned by companies represent 18 percent of the resale market, and employers may be willing to offer you a low down payment and low interest rate.

Lease with an Option to Buy

In this case, the buyer works out an agreement with the seller whereby the buyer commits to purchase the house in one year. The buyer signs a contract that fixes the price and obligation to pay. This is a good option when you are confident you can make the down payment by the following year. The other advantages of this strategy are that a portion of your monthly rent goes toward your down payment, and you gain valuable time to plan and accumulate savings.

Buy at a Builders' Condominium Auction

Desperate builders, eager to sell units, open up their units to auction. When they do, the buyer will benefit by checking with the realtor to see what similar units sold for and how many units are unsold. To learn about upcoming auctions check the real estate section of your newspaper and inquire with local agents about future auctions.

• A Closing Challenge

Now that I have taken you on my little journey into how to save, would you take me along with you?

Tell Me Without a doubt, many of you were sighing and shaking your heads about why I didn't include a certain savings concept that works well for you. Fortunately, there are many more ways to stretch a buck than the 52 identified in this book.

- What areas of savings did I leave out?
- How does savings occur in these areas?
- How do you personally benefit from saving this way?
- How much do you actually save over time?

Would you share your idea with me? Send your way to stretch a buck to:

52 Ways to Stretch a Buck
159 Via Serena
Rancho Santa Margarita, CA 92688

• Afterword

I trust that the life principles presented in *52 Ways to Stretch a Buck* will enrich your most important relationships. Some of us, however, are stuck in a cycle of spending and cannot turn it off. As a result, our most important relationships are suffering, and any relief we experience is quickly overwhelmed by guilt, shame, and conflict.

One challenge presented in this book is to take an inventory of our attitudes and behavior as well as our spending. Destructive spending habits often stem from inner turmoil. They are futile attempts to deal with unmet needs in our lives. And instead of the situation improving with time, inevitably it gets worse. Simple anecdotes cannot resolve these deeper issues.

The good news, however, is that even the most painful and desperate situation can be reversed with proper support and care. It takes courage to confront these issues and humility to share them with someone else. But people who understand the crisis you are facing can help. Life can begin again. For help call 1–800–227–LIFE.